# Mastering
# the Interview
# Process

Mikki J Bown

# CONTENTS

# INTRODUCTION

Congratulations and thank you for purchasing my book! You just took the first step towards preparing yourself to succeed in your next employment interview. Although interviewing can be intimidating it doesn't have to be debilitating. Preparation will ease your anxiety, boost your confidence, and increase your chances of landing your next job!

Voluntary or not, a job change usually kicks off the tedious job search process. No sugar-coating here. I have yet to meet anyone that enjoys searching for work. Spending countless hours scouring the Internet, want ads, and job boards then submitting numerous job-specific résumés is all done in hopes of securing the all-important interview.

More often than not people put more effort into the "job search" than the "job secure" which culminates with the interview. This is one of the biggest reasons people fail to secure employment. Just "showing up" for an interview could easily make a negative first impression. The key to having a successful interview, and leaving a positive lasting impression, is to actively and consciously participate in the interview.

I created this handbook after reading pages upon pages of material in interviewing books and Internet articles. Frequently I found I had to wade through lots of irrelevant verbiage to get to the useful material. Let's face it, interviewing is stressful enough. No one should have to spend a lot of frustrating hours searching for helpful information and tips. The material in this book is based on a vast amount of research, my many personal interviewing successes and failures, and years of experience as a Recruiter and hiring Manager.

Take a deep breath, get comfortable, and follow along as I walk you through an easy-to-follow process that will help you thoroughly prepare for, actively participate in, and successfully close your next interview.

# 1 PREPARATION RELEIVES APPREHENSION

Voluntary job changes occur for various reasons such as relocation, management restructuring, responsibility shifts, lack of challenge, or not feeling personally fulfilled. The unpleasant and sometimes gut-wrenching involuntary departure can happen as well. Whether voluntary or involuntary there is almost always a certain level of stress associated with a job change and the inevitable interviewing process.

Ah, the dreaded employment interview. For many people just the thought of this process makes their stomachs flutter and their palms sweat. Fortunately, the sometimes overwhelming anxiety associated with interviewing can easily be relieved by adequately preparing yourself for the process. Preparation will increase your confidence and decrease your apprehension.

In this chapter I'll identify the information and items you should assemble and have at your disposal during your interview.

## RESEARCH

Knowledge is power. Power instills confidence. Confidence is an essential part of every successful interview. This being said, it makes perfect sense that taking time to perform research before
your interview should be the first step in the interview preparation process.

## The Company

Gathering facts and information about the company you're going to interview with is crucial for a few very important reasons.

- **Is the company a good fit for you?**

  Familiarizing yourself with details about the company such as their history, growth, mission statement, core values, products, services, and divisions may help you decide whether the company is one that fits with your character and career goals. The office environment can have as much impact on job satisfaction, productivity, and length of employment as the position responsibilities or compensation.

  Selecting a company that compliments your individuality will help to ensure your success within the organization. Rarely do we find our perfect job, and sometimes a promising job turns out to be different than advertised. Thoroughly researching a company will decrease negative surprises and increase your chances of being satisfied with the position and environment.

- **Why do you want to work for the company?**

  Knowing at least three pieces of information about the company that either interests you or motivates you to work for them is essential for your interview. This information will prove indispensable when it comes time to answer this popular question asked during most interviews. I'll discuss this and other common interview questions later in the book.

### Getting to your Interview

Get complete directions to the interview location. Make a dry run the day before your actual interview date. Doing so will allow you to estimate your travel time based on the time of day, traffic load, and other potential travel obstacles. Give yourself extra time the day of your interview. Showing up late to your interview won't make a good first impression, but could make a bad lasting one.

Take a cell phone with you the day of your interview. Contact your interviewer immediately if you run into a traffic delay that could affect your ability to make your scheduled interview time. Although being tardy to your interview is not favorable, calling and explaining the reason for your delay is better than showing up late. Remember to silence your cell phone before entering the building.

## MATERIALS

Be organized. Collect and arrange all of the information and resources you'll need to complete the employment application form, and be effective in your interview. Remember that a successful interview requires you to be an active participant. Arm yourself with materials that will allow you to engage in a two-way information exchange about the company, position, and your qualifications for the job.

### Portfolio

A business portfolio conveys a professional image, provides a means to organize your interview materials, and often provides a boost in confidence. The cost of a portfolio varies based on material, capacity, and content. If funds aren't available to purchase a portfolio, ask family or friends if they have one you can borrow. If you can't acquire a portfolio, use some type of folder to hold your materials. Ensure they can't fall out.

### Research Materials

Although the information you collected about the company will demonstrate initiative and interest, sifting through the numerous papers you accumulated could make you appear unprepared and unorganized. Read through the company material you gathered. Filter out 5-6 facts or figures you find the most interesting. Legibly write this information on a sheet of paper so you can quickly refer to it during your interview. Put the paper in your portfolio or folder with your other interview material.

## Résumé

Have at least three complete copies of your résumé printed on quality résumé paper. You always want a copy to include with your application form, one for your interviewer, and one for yourself. If you know you'll be interviewing with more than one person, have a copy for each interviewer. If your résumé is more than one page don't staple or print it double-sided. Single-sided resumes are easier to read if the interviewer wants to look at your entire resume at once. They are also easier to photocopy. Use a paper-clip to attach multi-page resumes or just present them loosely to your interviewer. Be sure to have your pages in order.

## Job Posting

Print a copy of the original job posting that lists the job description, position responsibilities, and qualifications. If you're able to obtain more information about the position from the company website, print that as well. Make a table with two columns. Use the information you gathered to list the position's responsibilities and qualifications in one column. List your corresponding skills and experience in the other. Refer to this table during your interview to easily and clearly describe how your experience and abilities align with the position responsibilities.

## Employment History

Most application forms will have spaces for your last three or four employers. Be sure to have the information necessary to fully complete the employment section of the application form.

- Employer Name, Address, and Phone Number
- Supervisor Name, Title, and Phone Number
- Employment Dates
- Starting and Ending Salary
- Position Responsibilities

## Residence History

Many companies are now performing credit and background checks on prospective employees. One requirement for gathering this information could be a complete residence history for the past 10 years. Include the full street address, city, state, and zip code for each residence. Your authorization is required before a company can run any credit or background checks. Just be aware this is a possibility.

## References

Prepare a list of three professional and three personal references. Include the full name, title, complete address, telephone number, and years of acquaintance for each reference. Only select individuals that you know will provide positive feedback. You would be surprised by the number of times I called a personal reference to hear, "Who?" or to receive a negative reference.

Always contact your references before listing them on an application form or reference sheet. Provide them with some details about the company and position you are applying for. This will allow them to draw correlations between your skills and abilities and the position's requirements.

## Vocabulary List

Prepare a list of accurately spelled words you might use to complete the application form. This list includes some of the most commonly misspelled words on an application form.

- Accommodate
- Achieved
- Acquired
- Assembled
- Bachelor
- Business
- Experience

- Expertise
- Guarantee
- Negotiable
- Necessary
- Occasionally
- Preparation
- Satisfactory
- Successfully
- Volunteer

## Prepared Questions

As I previously stated, a successful interview is a two-way information exchange. During your interview you should perform two roles; the interviewee and the interviewer. Asking questions displays initiative and interest. Always ask at least three prepared questions relevant to the position or company at the end of your interview. Chapter 6 provides a few sample questions you might choose to ask your interviewer.

## Writing Instrument

Be sure to have two working black ink pens with you. Select pens that won't smudge if you run your hand across the ink. Click pens are preferable. You don't have to worry about searching for a dropped cap during your interview if your pen doesn't have one.

## Miscellaneous Items

Bring along any other information that is relevant or required for your interview. Here are a few examples.

- Copy of the letter or e-mail confirming the interview arrangements and interviewer's contact information.
- Letter or letters of recommendation. Limit these to three.

- Certification or Course Completion certificates relevant to the position you are applying for.
- Any other information you were requested to bring with you.

## INTERVIEW CHECKLIST

Preparation relieves apprehension so be sure you have the following items ready and organized before you head out the door for your interview.

- Company Address
- Directions
- Interview Materials
- Interviewer Contact Information
- Job History
- Job Posting
- Miscellaneous Materials
- Portfolio
- Prepared Questions
- References
- Research Materials
- Residence History
- Résumé
- Vocabulary list
- Writing Instruments

Don't let the list overwhelm or defeat you. Take your time to do the research and gather all the information. You might actually feel a sense of relief once you start preparing. Remember, knowledge is power and power instills confidence. Confidence will help you succeed in your interview.

## 2 IMAGE EQUALS IMPRESSION

There's an old saying that goes something like this, "Everyone appears intelligent until they open their mouth." Many times an initial judgment is made about a person within the first 60 seconds of a meeting. A professional image can greatly influence a first impression. The following tips can help establish a professional presence by displaying confidence, competence, and a strong character before you ever speak a word.

### APPEARANCE

We learned at a very early age that how we're perceived has a lot to do with the first impression we make. The first impression you make to a perspective employer can greatly affect their impression of you and consequently, positively or negatively, influence the outcome of your interview before it even begins. Dressing appropriately for your job interview is crucial to presenting a professional image suitable for the prospective work environment.

For many companies long gone are the days of suit and tie environments. A business casual dress code is now more commonplace. If you dress too formal for your interview you might come across as rigid or stuffy. If you dress too casual you might give the impression that you don't take the interview seriously. Contact the Human Resources department prior to your interview and ask about the company dress code. Always dress a step above the stated dress code. If you're not able to obtain dress code information play it safe. Choose clothing that presents a professional image and fits you well. Some great advice I received early in my career was this, "Dress for the job you want, not the job you have."

Keep body jewelry to a minimum and cover all body art unless these items are considered acceptable for the position you're interviewing for. Don't wear perfume, cologne, or strong smelling deodorants. Avoid smoking in your interview clothes. Many people are allergic to certain scents, and some may find particular smells offensive. It's important to remember that what smells good to you may not be pleasing to your interviewer.

## Men

- Wear a well-tailored suit, preferably blue or black. If a suit is not available or not appropriate for the work environment wear a coordinating sport coat and slacks. At a minimum wear slacks, a dress shirt, and tie. Wear a leather belt.

- Press your shirt and crease your slacks.

- Make sure your tie isn't frayed.

- Polish your leather shoes and replace worn laces.

- Hair should be neat and groomed.

- Nails should be trimmed and clean.

- Facial hair should be trimmed and neat.

## Women

- Wear a classic suit, dress, or blouse with skirt or slacks. Stick with basic colors such as blue, black, gray, or burgundy. Don't wear provocative clothing. Miniskirts, sheer or low cut blouses, and stretch pants are inappropriate for interviewing.

- Wear closed toe shoes with preferably a 1-1 ½ inch heel or flats. Open toe shoes might be acceptable depending on the workplace environment. If you wear open toe shoes be sure to have toenails painted with a clear or neutral color.

- Hair should be neat and styled. Wear it so you don't have to brush it out of your face during the interview.

- Nails should be trimmed and polished with a clear or neutral color.

## BODY LANGUAGE

Your body language from eye contact to how you sit in a chair can influence your interviewer's perception of you. Proper body language can portray energy, interest, and confidence. Matching the posture and speaking style of your interviewer will help to build rapport. Building rapport could easily give you an advantage over other qualified candidates.

### Pleasantries

Be polite and courteous to everyone you encounter from the time you enter the parking lot until the time you leave. You never know when you might encounter someone involved in the interview or hiring process. Never forget to offer a simple "thank you" to everyone providing assistance. Smile, smile, smile.

### Eye Contact

Make eye contact with everyone you meet from the minute you walk through the door until you leave the building. The amount of eye contact to maintain with an individual can be a delicate balance. Research suggests maintaining eye contact between 60-70 percent of the time during a meeting is ideal for building rapport. Too much could make the other person uncomfortable. Too little could be construed as avoidance or a lack of confidence. Practicing eye contact is very important because the right amount of eye contact will convey confidence, interest, and respect.

During your interview it is acceptable to look away from your interviewer when formulating an answer to a question. Never look down at your feet as though searching for an answer. Quickly return to your interviewer to continue the discussion. Be careful not to turn your eye contact into a staring contest. Remember to blink. Don't hesitate to periodically look away from your interviewer or down to your notes for a quick break but don't start looking around the room. The key is to stay engaged in the conversation.

## Posture

When standing, stand tall with your back straight and your head up. Don't look at your feet thus avoiding eye contact. You might want to consider standing while you're waiting for your interviewer. This will prevent your clothes from wrinkling and allow you to greet your interviewer with the presence of a peer.

When sitting, maintain a straight posture while keeping your shoulders relaxed. Don't slouch. Place your elbows on the arms of the chair or at your sides. You might find it comfortable to loosely clasp your fingers and place your hands on your lap. Never cross your arms while standing or sitting. This type of body language is often interpreted as closed-off or defensive.

Don't cross your legs when seated. Doing so can make it difficult to adjust your posture and body language. Crossing your legs could also relax you and cause you to slouch in your chair. Keep your feet flat on the floor, or cross one foot behind the other at the ankle.

Keep hand gestures to a minimum as this can be distracting to your interviewer and take attention away from what you're saying. Wringing your hands or twirling your thumbs might be perceived as a sign of nervousness. Fiddling with a pen, cracking your knuckles, and tapping your fingers on your portfolio should also be avoided.

## PROFESSIONALISM

### Arrival Times

Arrive approximately 30 minutes before your scheduled interview time. Take a few minutes to emotionally prepare for your interview, review your material, and visit the restroom. Do a final check of your appearance.

Announce your arrival to the Receptionist approximately 15 minutes before your scheduled interview time. This will allow sufficient time to begin completing the employment application form if one is required. Announcing your arrival earlier is not recommended. If they wanted to interview you 30 minutes earlier they would've scheduled it for then.

## Handshake

Whether you are male or female, always present a firm handshake. Your handshake can say a lot about you. Studies show there is a significant correlation between the features of a firm handshake such as strength, duration, and grip and a favorable first impression.

A neutral handshake with both hands coming in from each side is preferable. If your interviewer places his or her hand on top you can gently rotate your hand to the side but be careful. Forcing your hand on top of the handshake or placing your free hand on top of the interviewer's hand could be perceived as aggressive.

## Introductions

Typically the person leading the interview will do the introductions and initiate the handshake. If for some reason your interviewer doesn't extend their hand to you, take the initiative. Offer your hand when introducing yourself. Be aware of your hand placement in the handshake.

Continue standing until you are offered a seat. If you have an option, select a firm chair over a plush chair. This will allow you to easily modify your posture throughout the interview. Sit at a slight angle to your interviewer. This can make eye contact easier to establish. It might also soften the communication exchange.

Hold mock introductions with friends and family. This is a great way to work on eye contact and posture. The more you practice the more comfortable you'll become with the process. Shake hands with various people. How do the different types of grips make you feel? Use that information to gauge the firmness of your handshake.

# 3 THE APPLICATION FORM

The application form may be one of the most selective screening tools used by a prospective employer. It can be used to see how well an individual follows instructions as well as determine neatness, thoroughness, and the spelling and writing abilities of a candidate. It isn't uncommon for staff in personnel offices to review an application form, and then make judgments regarding the applicant's qualifications for a position prior to ever meeting the candidate.

Completing the application form accurately, completely, neatly, and truthfully can greatly increase your chances of getting an interview if one hasn't already been scheduled, or landing the job you are preparing to interview for. Consider the following suggestions to help you effectively complete the application form.

## BE PREPARED

Don't make assumptions. If you're filling out the application form at the prospective employer's site, don't assume they'll have a phone book or dictionary available for your use as this is often not the case. Be sure to have the following prepared information with you to expedite filling out the application form.

## Résumé

Use a copy of your résumé as a resource. Do not write "See Résumé" on the application form even though you will be including a copy. Just referencing the hard copy is not an acceptable practice because your résumé could become separated from your application form.

## Employer Information

Most employers will be interested in your last 3-4 jobs or 10-15 years of work experience. If you've only worked for one or two employers then that is all you would list. If you've had more employers than space, list the jobs that are relevant to the position you are applying for. When applying for your first professional job keep in mind that babysitting, fund raising for school, yard maintenance, and other revenue-generating activities all count as employment.

If a previous employer is no longer in business list the address the business occupied during your employment. Write a brief sentence stating that the company no longer exists, and provide a short explanation. Using your previously prepared employment history reference sheet will assist with quickly completing this section of the application form.

## Supervisor Information

Use your reference sheet to list the complete name, title, and phone number of your direct Supervisor at each employer listed on the application form. If the individual is no longer in the position write a few words explaining the situation.

## Vocabulary List

Bring along your prepared vocabulary list. It is acceptable to use your phone to look up words, but this can take more time than you have to complete the application. If you're unsure of the spelling of a word and it's not on your list then definitely look it up. Take every precaution not to misspell any words on the application form.

## Residence History

Don't forget to bring your prepared residence history. This will make completing this portion of the application form quick and easy.

## Job Posting

The job posting will provide the position title, department, position responsibilities, and possibly the salary range.

## COMPLETING THE APPLICATION FORM

If possible, request two copies of the application form. It's always good to have a spare in case you make mistakes. Scribbling out or striking through an answer does not portray accuracy. Never use white-out to make a correction.

Read the application and instructions completely before you begin. This is not a timed exam. Announcing yourself to the Receptionist 15 minutes before your interview and having your prepared information with you should give you sufficient time to complete the application.

Complete the application form as accurately, completely, neatly, and most importantly truthfully as possible following these suggested Dos and Don'ts.

## Do

- Make sure your handwriting is legible and clear. The information is useless if no one can read it.
- Avoid using abbreviations.
- Write "Open" or "Negotiable" in the Desired Salary field. It is often best to wait until you hear more about the position and responsibilities before specifying a salary requirement. If you know what the salary range is for the position, and you have a number within the range that you must have to accept the position then write it down. If you do this, keep in mind it can be very difficult to ask for a higher salary than the one you specified.

- Positively explain, without going into too much detail, any gaps in your employment history.

- Include with your application a copy of your résumé and any other documents such as certificates, awards, and letters of recommendation that are relevant to the position. Be careful not to overdo it.

- Check your application very carefully for spelling, punctuation, and grammatical errors. If you find any errors make note of them, and fill out the second application form with the correct information.

- Request a copy of the completed application form. This is a not common practice so don't be offended if you receive a puzzled look. Explain that you prefer to have a copy in case any questions arise about the information you provided.

**Don't**

- Leave any items or sections incomplete on the application form. Write "N/A" or "Not Applicable" if a something doesn't apply to you. White space may lead the individual reviewing your application to believe the section or question was overlooked.

- Use negative words or statements when describing your reason for leaving your current or previous employer. Stick to facts. Leave out personal feelings or vendettas.

- Lie on any part of your application. Employment verification and a possible background check will most likely be performed.

- Rush. Take your time to completely fill out the application form. If you're not able to complete the application before your interview, simply take it with you. You can finish it afterwards.

- Forget to sign your application form.

The same principles apply if you fill out the application form on-line. Although completing the application form on-line may hide your less than stellar penmanship, spelling, punctuation, and grammatical errors are still a concern. Review your on-line application thoroughly before you submit it.

# 4 SET THE TONE

Many people mentally set the tone for their interview before ever entering the interviewing site. The problem is, many times they set the wrong tone and subsequently aren't successful in their interview. How do you set the right tone? It all comes down to one word, confidence. If you have confidence in your qualifications, appearance, and preparation, that conviction will emanate throughout your interview and positively influence your interview experience.

Often times an interview is scheduled weeks after you initially apply for a position. If this is the case, you might need a little motivation to mentally prepare yourself to set the right tone for your interview. To do this, simply remind yourself what interested or excited you about the position in the first place.

Whatever your reason or motivation for applying for the job, you need to appear genuinely excited about the opportunity during your interview. If you don't, it could be very difficult to convince your interviewer that you are the right candidate for the job.

Employers want employees that are outgoing, energetic, driven, motivated, and pleasant to work with. Be enthusiastic, cheerful, interested, assertive, and confident during your interview but be cautious. Confidence can border on arrogance and arrogance is one characteristic you want to leave at home.

## EMOTIONAL PREPARATON

It's the day of your interview. Being nervous is common and expected whether it's your first or fifteenth interview. Arriving a little early and performing a relaxation activity might help to ease your anxiety. You could perform these activities prior to leaving for your interview, but many times anxiety doesn't surface until you're on your way to the interview site.

As stated previously, arrive approximately 30 minutes before your scheduled interview. Allow yourself a few minutes to do one of the following relaxation activities. Don't do anything that could impair your speech or ability to think clearly.

- Read something to clear your mind.
- Take a short walk.
- Listen to music.
- Smell a calming scent like lavender or lemon.

Most importantly, remind yourself that the employer has already decided you are worth meeting. You have the skills they are looking for or you wouldn't be waiting for your interview.

## KNOW THE PURPOSE

Whether you're interviewing with an individual from Human Resources, the department manager, or a potential co-worker they're all looking for an answer to the same question, "Why should we hire you?" Be constantly aware of this and tailor your responses accordingly.

Your preliminary research of the company and position should provide you with enough information to gauge your ability to fit into the organization and successfully fulfil the position responsibilities. Never hesitate to interview for a position that you aren't 100% qualified for. If you possess 75% of the qualifications the employer is seeking, you can fill in the missing 25% with enthusiasm and aptitude.

Always go into an interview believing and projecting that this is the job you've always wanted. Convince everyone you interview with that you're the candidate they've been looking for. It's always better to be offered a job and turn it down, than not be offered the job at all.

Don't forget that you too have a purpose in attending the interview. Your purpose is to determine if the position is a good fit for your skills, abilities, and personality, to state your qualifications for the position, and to ultimately ask for the job.

## ADAPT TO THE ENVIRONMENT

Be aware of the interview environment and adapt to your surroundings. If you're fortunate enough to meet in your interviewer's office, look around. Make note of pictures, awards, or sports memorabilia. Use your surroundings to develop commonalities with your interviewer. Connecting with your interviewer on a personal level might make the interview environment feel more comfortable, and could positively influence the interview process.

### Building Rapport

Building rapport is an essential part of your interview. Follow your interviewer's behavior throughout the interview. Doing so will allow you to establish a common tempo, and could possibly make the interview flow more smoothly. If he or she sits up straight, leans toward the table, or relaxes back in their chair, loosely mimic the behavior. The key word is loosely. Make subtle changes in your posture to match that of your interviewer when it's your turn to speak.

Try and match voice characteristics. Listen to your interviewer's pitch, tempo, and emotion. Try to briefly emulate it the best you can. Pay attention to the type of language being used. Is he or she using words or phrases associated with sports, architecture, or nature? If so, try and use a few similar words or phrases.

While making slight adjustments in your posture, tone, or language to establish a connection with your interview, always remain mindful of maintaining a professional presence. If you catch yourself becoming too comfortable regain your composure. Never lose sight of the fact that you are in an interview not a social situation.

## Refreshments

Don't accept an initial offer for a refreshment. There is no reason to take a chance of spilling something on you, the floor or the table. If you're in a long interview or interviewing with more than one person, it is appropriate to accept a refreshment during a break. Always opt for water. If you need to use the restroom, politely request a break between interviewers.

## Taking Notes

There is nothing wrong with taking notes during an interview as long as it doesn't interfere with your eye contact or focus. Before pulling out your paper and pen you might say something like, "It's important for me to capture the highlights of our interview, do you mind if I take notes?"

Don't be surprised if your interviewer appears confused. Displaying this type of courtesy is rare. It will definitely make a positive impression. Don't try and capture everything that's said. Focusing too much on taking notes could distract you from the conversation.

Use the information covered in this chapter to set the tone for some mock interviews. Watch the body language of your friend or family member. Try to loosely mimic it without them noticing. Can you match their language, tempo and tone? Building rapport with your interviewer is essential. Continue practicing these skills until you feel comfortable with the process.

# 5 INTERVIEW QUESTIONS AND ANSWERS

Your interview will most likely include a question and answer session. Questions might be posed throughout the interview or at the end. This is a crucial part of the interview process. It is one of the most effective ways for an employer to find out about you as an individual, your qualifications for the position, your ability to think on your feet, and your interest in the company and position.

This is often the "make or break" part of the interview. Providing clear and concise answers are vital to your interviewing success.

## FORMULATING YOUR RESPONSES

Use the following tips to formulate your responses to interview questions.

- During the interview you should talk approximately one-third of the time and never more than half.

- Practice good listening skills. You can't provide a complete answer without knowing the complete question.

- Limit your responses to 1½-2 minutes. Your interviewer's attention will begin to fade after approximately 90 seconds.

- Stay focused on the question. Be specific with your answers. Often times a candidate will get off topic when answering a question and end up providing irrelevant information. If you sense yourself starting to wander during your response wrap it up quickly. Pull your interviewer back into the conversation by saying something like, "My apologies. I believe I got a little off topic. Did I provide enough information to thoroughly answer your question?"

- Watch your interviewer. If his or her eyes start to wander or they adjust their posture wrap up your response. Again, you can re-engage your interviewer by asking him or her a question.

- Do not answer a question with a simple yes or no. Always provide a brief explanation.

- Do not provide information that could be perceived as negative. Make all of your responses positive.

- Do not divulge personal information that could be discriminated against. Yes, this is illegal but it happens. Save details about your political affiliations, religious beliefs, family, children, and even pets until after you have the job.

- If you're unsure if your response was sufficient, ask your interviewer a question something like, "Is this the type of information you were looking for?" or "Does that sufficiently answer your question?"

## COMMON INTERVIEW QUESTIONS

Although it's impossible to look into a crystal ball and know every question you might be presented with during your interview, you can be certain you'll receive a few of the following common interview questions. As previously discussed, preparation is the key to feeling confident and relieving anxiety. Preparation will allow you to calmly and competently answer any interview question.

Prepare your responses to these common interview questions. Write them down and practice reciting them. Talking in front of a mirror or role-playing with friends and family are both excellent ways of tackling fears of public speaking and streamlining your responses. You want your responses to be casual and fluid. Be careful not to come across as though you're reading from a script.

## Why did you leave your last position?

If you're still employed you would speak to why you are seeking opportunities outside of your current employer. Be very careful with this question. Your answer could give your interviewer insight into your motivation, temperament, and commitment to working through employment difficulties.

Even if you absolutely hated your job responsibilities, coworkers or manager don't express it. There is no place in an interview for negativity. You might say you left because you weren't being challenged, and although you expressed this to your immediate supervisor your responsibilities didn't change. This shows you took initiative to try and improve the situation instead of just getting frustrated and leaving.

Another reason might be that you felt you had accomplished all you could in your current role, and there were limited opportunities within the organization that aligned with your skills and career goals. This shows you looked within the organization for continued employment opportunities prior to looking outside the company.

Finally, you might say that your position responsibilities changed after you were hired. You could mention how you desire to continually strengthen and build your existing skills as well as learn new ones, but unfortunately your current or previous position no longer provided that opportunity.

If your reason for leaving your current position is due to relocation, a desire to change careers, company downsizing or you have always wanted to work for the company you are interviewing with, tell them so. These reasons for job or career change are rarely scrutinized.

Whatever your response is to this question, be ready to back it up with more information. A few sentences should suffice. Remember, never provide more detail then necessary. You don't want to give your interviewer information that could be perceived as unfavorable. Practice this question until you feel comfortable with your response.

## Why would we want to hire you?

What they are really asking is, "What do you have to offer our organization?"

Here is your chance to sell yourself. Take full advantage of this question. Many people tend to use phrases like "highly motivated" or "team player" when describing their qualifications. Steer away from these types of generic statements. Set yourself apart from other applicants by summarizing your individual qualifications and drawing parallels to the requirements of the position you're interviewing for. When formulating your answer ask yourself, "What qualifications do I possess that make me unique?"

## Why do you want to work here?

What they are really asking is, "What do you know about our company and the position?"
Don't make the mistake of providing a generalized answer. Doing so might give the impression that you didn't research the company thus displaying a lack of initiative and enthusiasm about the position. Use the information you gathered while performing your research to formulate a detailed answer demonstrating how your personality, career goals, skills, and experience match the company's values, needs, and position responsibilities.

Be sure to mention desirable characteristics about the company and position that are not or were not available at your current or previous employer. This helps establish justification for seeking a new opportunity.

## What is your greatest strength?

What they are really asking is, "Are you confident in your abilities?"

Take this opportunity to state one or two of your strengths. They might include strong verbal and written communication skills, the ability to motivate people around you, or effective multi-tasking skills. Be sure to explain how these strengths allowed you to succeed at work or in a personal situation, and how they would allow you to successfully perform the position's responsibilities. Don't use this as an opportunity to flatter yourself. The key is to exhibit humility not arrogance.

## What is your greatest weakness?

What they are really asking is, "Are you honest?"

Everyone has weaknesses. You know it and so does your interviewer. The key to successfully answering this question is to be honest. Talk about how you recognized a weakness and have or are currently working to improve in that area. Stay away from personal characteristics such as short-tempered, anxious, or unmotivated and concentrate on personal skills such as organization, communication, delegation, or prioritization.

## Where do you want to be in two, five or 10 years?

What they are really asking is, "Do you have any ambitions or aspirations?"

Be reasonable based on your experience and skills. Your answer should depict your focus, dedication, and ambition. Be careful not to give the impression that you want to move up the corporate ladder too quickly. Although many companies desire to promote from within, you don't want your interviewer to feel as though you only see this position as a means of getting your foot in the door.

A safe response would be, "It's difficult to say where I want to be in the future without knowing more about other positions within this or other departments. I do know I'm looking for a company where I can establish myself and build my career."

## Describe a problem situation and how you resolved it.

What they are really asking is, "Can you think on your feet and take responsibility to resolve an issue?"

This can be a difficult question to answer, particularly if you have limited or no professional work experience. Even though you might not have had the challenge of facing and resolving problem situations at work, you've probably encountered them in other areas of your life.

Maybe you experienced difficulties such as finding enough time to study while in school, facing the consequences of a traffic violation, or dealing with disciplining defiant children. No matter what the problem was, describe the steps you took to resolve the situation. Doing so will demonstrate your ability to accept responsibility and mentally work through the steps necessary to resolve the problem on your own. Telling a story can become lengthy so be conscious of the time you spend answering this question.

**What type of experience do you have with…?**

During the interview you will most likely be asked to describe your experience working with certain technologies, applications or machines associated with the position responsibilities. If you're asked if you have experience with something and you don't, don't respond with a simple, "No." Start your response with, "I haven't had the opportunity…"

Let's say you're asked if you have experience with Microsoft Excel and you don't or you have very little. A better response would be, "I haven't had the opportunity to work with Excel but I'm certain my experience working with other Microsoft products would allow me to quickly become proficient with the application."

**What type of salary are you looking for?**

This question is one many people find the most difficult to answer.

You don't want to ask for too much money putting yourself outside of the salary range nor do you want to ask for too little shortchanging your qualifications. It's a good idea to decide on your bottom line or "must have" compensation before your interview.

The ideal situation would be for your interviewer to present you with the salary range at some point during the interview. Unfortunately, this doesn't happen very often. When it doesn't, there are two possible avenues to pursue when tackling this difficult question; Preparation and Avoidance.

- **Preparation**. Prior to your interview contact the Human Resources department of the prospective employer and inquire about the salary range for the position. If they aren't willing or are unable to provide you with the information do some research. Use salary tools available on the Internet to get a general idea of the industry-specific salary range in your geographic area based on your experience level and qualifications.

- **Avoidance**. You can avoid directly answering the question and turn the responsibility of making an initial offer back to your interviewer. This can be a tricky process. You don't want to turn a compensation discussion into a situation resembling that of purchasing a used car. The following responses can be very effective at redirecting the salary question.

  - "In what range do you typically pay someone with my experience and qualifications?"

  - "Since I'm not aware of how this position is valuated within your organization, would you be willing to share the salary range for this position with me?"

  - "I prefer to postpone talking about compensation until we both feel we have enough information to agree that there is mutual interest in my candidacy for the position."

If you try one of these redirects and it doesn't work, your interviewer may come back with another request for your desired salary. Be prepared to provide a number or at least a range that you would be comfortable accepting. Never say, "I don't know" or I'm not sure."

If you know your minimum acceptable hourly rate or salary figure is X then ask for X+10% to 15%. It is best to leave room for negotiation if an offer is made.

# 6 WRAP IT UP

You made it through the bulk of your interview. You truthfully and concisely answered all of the interview questions, and you provided detailed information about your skills, employment and education. Based on this, you feel your contribution to the interview is over. Believing this statement to be true might possibly be the biggest mistake you could make during the interview.

## INTERVIEW YOUR INTERVIEWER

You captivated your interviewer by displaying ambition, interest, and motivation. You skillfully demonstrated how your qualifications directly correspond with the position requirements. You even successfully dealt with the salary question. But if you don't have any questions for your interviewer at the end of the interview, you quite possibly just closed an open door.

One of the biggest disappointments an interviewer faces in an interview is when they ask the candidate if they have any questions and the response they receive is, "No, I don't. You provided all of the information I was hoping to obtain from our interview today. I'm very excited about the position." What only minutes before could have been construed as "the perfect interview" now has a major shortcoming exposed.

Not asking any questions is often perceived as a lack of interest. It is imperative to pose a minimum of three questions to your interviewer at the end of the interview to cement your interest in the company and position. Have a list of at least six prepared questions. This provides a buffer in case your interviewer answers some of the questions on your list during the interview. Ask questions specific to the company and position. Do not ask questions about salary, benefits, or advancement opportunities. The following are samples of questions you may choose to ask your interviewer.

- What are the greatest challenges of this position?

- What are some of the immediate objectives you would like to see accomplished in this position?

- What would you like to see done differently by the person who fills this position?

- How is someone evaluated in this position?

- Why is the position open?

- How many times has this position been open in the past five years?

## CLOSE THE INTERVIEW

Many times people leave an interview without achieving their primary purpose for attending the interview, asking for the job. Even if the position isn't your ideal job, follow through and close the interview. Reiterate your interest in the position, and ask for the job. Situations and attitudes change. What might not seem like an ideal position today could become more appealing in the future. Keep in mind that you can always decline an offer if one is extended.

Closing the interview can be a daunting process for many people. Intimidation, awkwardness, and fear are emotions often associated with the closing process. The primary reason these emotions surface is because most individuals feel they are in the interview to provide information. They don't think about asking for anything, especially employment, but isn't that why you're there? Your closing statement should accomplish the following objectives.

- Demonstrate initiative, ambition, and a desire for the position.

- Reiterate why you are the perfect candidate for the job.

- Prompt your interviewer to divulge any questions or hesitations he or she might have regarding your ability to fit into the organization, or to perform the position's responsibilities.

Here is an example of an effective closing statement.

"We've discussed in great detail the position and my qualifications for the job. I am very interested in the position, and excited about the possibility of joining the organization. Do you have any questions or concerns that would keep you from offering me this position?"

If your interviewer expresses any hesitations or concerns take the opportunity to address them immediately. This is your opportunity to leave a lasting impression. Once you address any potential obstacles, or if your interviewer doesn't express any, tell them you appreciate the time they spent with you today and you look forward to the next stage in the hiring process. This puts the ball back in their court. If you weren't handed one at the beginning of the interview, ask your interviewer for his or her business card before leaving.

## PROPER FOLLOW-UP

The interview may be over but your work is still not done. The job search isn't finished until you've been offered the position, negotiated your compensation, accepted the job, and received your offer letter. Here are a few more tasks you should complete to increase your chances of being offered the position.

Send a thank you note to everyone you interviewed with. This is the most overlooked and underutilized step in the interview process. The note should be comprised of a few sentences thanking your interviewer for their time, expressing your interest in the position, and stating that you will follow-up in a few days. Although email is easier, a handwritten note delivered to the office will really set you apart from other candidates.

Follow-up with your interviewer 2-3 days after your interview. Inquire about the status of the hiring process, and ask if you can provide any further information that would be helpful in securing the position. Follow-up again in 6-7 days unless you're instructed otherwise. Continually follow-up every 3-4 days until you're offered the position or informed that the position has been filled. Persistence keeps your name in front of the interviewer.

Even if you think you nailed the interview, and the responses you're receiving from the interviewer or Human Resources about your possible selection for the position are positive, DO NOT stop interviewing for other positions until you have a signed offer letter. I can't list the number of times a candidate thought the job was "in the bag" to find out another person was selected.

If you're not offered the position inquire as to why. Most often you'll get a generic response that another candidate was more qualified, but there might be times when you'll actually receive information that can assist you in future interviews. You won't know if you don't ask.

## ACCEPTING AN OFFER

Negotiating pay can be intimidating but never feel pressured to accept an offer as soon as one is made. Most employers won't make their first offer their best offer. Tell them how excited you are about the offer and request a day or two to review the responsibilities and compensation.

Salary isn't the only negotiable component of a job offer. Many companies are often held to defined salary ranges and mid-point restrictions. Because of this, fronted vacation days, company stock offerings, and sign-on bonuses are becoming more commonplace as part of a complete compensation package.

Don't hesitate to counter an offer. Be reasonable in your request, and be prepared to justify why you feel you warrant the additional money or benefits. The company already made the decision they want to hire you. Negotiating your compensation package is an acceptable and often expected part of the hiring process.

# 7 ONLINE RESOURCES

Searching for a job today is much easier than it was 10 years ago. The Internet contains numerous websites dedicated to the job search and application process. Whether you're looking for your first job, or a seasoned professional desiring a career change, you'll be able to find a website specific to your situation.

The following websites might prove useful when contemplating career choices, searching for jobs, investigating salaries, performing company research, and setting up a free email account you can use to apply for jobs and correspond with prospective employers.

## CAREER INFORMATION SITES

- Advice.CareerBuilder.com
- CareerOneStop.org
- Monster.com

## JOB SEARCH SITES

### Communications and Media

- CommunicationsJobs.net
- JournalismJobs.com

- MediaBistro.com
- TalentZoo.com

## General

- CarrerBuilder.com
- Craigslist.org
- Glassdoor.com
- Indeed.com
- Monster.com
- SimplyHired.com
- TheLadders.com
- USAJobs.gov

## Healthcare

- HealthcareJobsite.com
- HealthJobsNationwide.com
- MiracleWorkers.com

## Hospitality

- Culintro.com
- HCareers.com
- HospitalityOnline.com
- JobsOnTheMenu.com

## Finance Industry

- Doostang.com
- eFinancialCareers.com
- Financialjobsweb.com

### Technical Jobs

- Crunchboard.com
- Dice.com
- StackOverflow.com
- TechCareers.com

### Temporary Jobs

- Flexjobs.com
- Odesk.com
- Snagajob.com

## SALARY SITES

- Monster.salary.com
- PayScale.com
- Salary.com
- SalaryExpert.com

## BUSINESS INFORMATION SITES

- Business.com
- Hoovers.com
- Vault.com

## FREE EMAIL PROVIDERS

- Gmail.com
- GMX.com
- Outlook.com
- Yahoo.com

# CONCLUSION

The Bureau of Labor Statics stated that the average worker stays at each of his or her jobs for 4.4 years. According to the "Multiple Generations @ Work" survey conducted by Future Workplace, ninety-one percent of Millennials (born between 1977-1997) expect to stay in a job for less than three years. Based on these numbers you could easily have 15-20 jobs during your lifetime.

Each job change will most likely require you to participate in the interview and application process. Becoming proficient at interviewing will prove essential to securing and maintaining gainful employment throughout your job changes. I hope the information I provided in my book will help you thoroughly prepare for, actively participate in, and successfully close all of your interviews.

www.ingramcontent.com/pod-product-compliance
Lightning Source LLC
Chambersburg PA
CBHW072314200526
45168CB00014B/1511